And When the Sun Rises...

2017 West Florida Literary Federation Student Poetry Contest Winners

The West Florida Literary Federation
Escambia County Student Poetry Contest
is held annually as a combined effort involving:

West Florida Literary Federation
Pensacola Cultural Center
400 South Jefferson Street, Suite 210
Pensacola, FL 32501-5902
www.wflf.org

Escambia County School District
Escambia County, FL
www.escambia.k12.fl.us

Escambia County Catholic and Christian Schools
Escambia County, FL

Pensacola Public Library
200 West Gregory Street
Pensacola, FL 32502
www.mywfpl.com

Books-a-Million
6235 North Davis Highway
Pensacola, FL 32504
www.booksamillion.com

My thanks to everyone who worked tirelessly
behind the scenes keeping me organized. There
are simply too many to name and if I name one,
I would have to name you all. Suffice to say, this
contest would not be successful without the
dedication and enthusiasm of those who continue
to make it happen every year.
-Susan Lewis

TABLE OF CONTENTS

Introduction
...*from Andrea Walker*
Vice President
West Florida Literary Federation

Introduction
...*from Susan A. Lewis*
Student Poetry Director
West Florida Literary Federation

<u>2017 Winners</u>

A note
from Andrea Walker
Vice President
West Florida Literary Federation

Poetry probably serves a different purpose for every person, but one thing is certain. Getting one's poetry published is an accomplishment and milestone. The work you are holding in your hands manifests the growing minds of our future.

Poetry is powerful in the hands and minds of those who use it, whether as a tool of self-expression, to reach others, or to promote a cause. Readers, as well as writers, can find comfort and empathy in poetry. While history boasts many great poets, most writers of verse do not achieve fame or wealth. But what we get from poetry as individuals and as a society is immeasurable. Poetry touches people and changes lives. Young and old alike share feelings of sadness as well as joy. People rejoice in the beauty of nature and love, cry over tragedies, and take action in response to political poetry. Readers and listeners alike empathize with the speakers of poems.

While analysis and interpretation of poetry is stimulating and valid, one's personal response may be different from what the poet intended. Good for you. The poem has reached someone else and served yet another purpose. When reading the work of great poets, it's easy to accept what critics have told us about the work. Sometimes, however, a great poem means something to a student that no critic has ever suggested. At that point, the poem itself has grown and given the reader expanded insight the poet may not have considered.

Writing poetry serves as catharsis and at times expresses the sublime. The art of writing is not only challenging, but also painful at times. Writing enables one to express emotion in concrete terms and share it, which in turn helps others understand. In education, we are experiencing a lack of emphasis on arts. Yet, we live in a world where self-expression is encouraged. The human condition demands that we create.

With great honor, I introduce this collection of student poetry. I applaud Susan Lewis for the heart, soul and sweat she puts into this project each year. I applaud the teachers who make this program accessible to their students. I applaud the parents who encourage their children and who sometimes watch them blossom into new areas. Most of all, I applaud the students who put their hearts into their work. Their poetry is fruit of planted seeds. I hope they continue to nurture their talents and enjoy the process.

Andrea Walker
VP WFLF
Poetry co-editor Panoplyzine.com

A note
from Susan Lewis
Student Poetry Director

Fellow poets,

After the emotional weight of last year's theme, I knew what had to follow would have to be a 'coming out of the darkness'. So that is exactly what I chose.

As the director of this contest, I am aware that a theme isn't simply a theme. It becomes a discussion with your parent, a topic in the classroom, writing exercises, dreams and maybe a few disagreements over what is or is not appropriate.

Poets cannot just sit down and write.

Poets linger over topics. They observe the nature of the subject from every possible angle.

The Sun wasn't the Sun this year.

It was gaseous and glorious. He was emboldened with a fiery anger while also sullen and misunderstood. She was strong, stoic...steady, unlike her lazy lunar brother, always hiding in the dark. The Sun was all things under itself and more.

I am always in awe of you all and I am always so proud.

*Thank you for
protecting my art,*

-Susan A. Lewis

WFLF Student Poetry Director

10

1st–2nd Grade Division

GRADES 1 – 2
1st PLACE

Natalie Jackson
Grade 2, Episcopal Day School
Ms. Caldwell, Teacher

At the Beach

Birds are chirping
The sun is rising today
Bumblebees are buzzing
What an awesome day
Butterflies around me
Feet are in the sand
What a beautiful land
Going up and down
Going all around
Sun glaring at me
Look what I can see
Flowers waving in the wind
I have a grin
The light on my face
With a salty taste
Happily a new day

GRADES 1 – 2
2nd PLACE

Jacob Weekley
Grade 2, Episcopal Day School
Ms. Garner, Teacher

Dark and Light

One day there was Dark and Light.
Dark spent time resting
Light spent time painting.
One day, Light got tired of working so hard
day and night while Dark just rested.
They got mad at each other.
Dark's clouds filled the sky as his lightning
shattered the ground.
Light painted a shield
of black, grey and purple.
The gods showed up and said
"this is nonsense!"
The Sun came up,
Dark and Light were friends again.

GRADES 1 – 2
3rd PLACE

Gus Brown
Grade 2, Episcopal Day School
Ms. Caldwell, Teacher

Spring

The sun is rising
it is so beautiful.
It looks like a huge orange blob floating
around in the sky.
Flowers are blooming all around.
Blue flowers, red and yellow flowers,
they all look so different.
I love the look of these outstanding flowers.
The sky is getting gray and black.
I think it might rain.
Plip plop plip plop – it's raining!
Get inside!
Zap zap lightning and thunder!
The rain has stopped.
The sun is coming back up.
The birds are chirping.
I see all different colorful birds.
The birds are peeping and flying around.
The birds little sing song makes me smile.
I love the beautiful sight of Spring.

GRADES 1 – 2
HONORABLE MENTION

Havanna Walker
Grade 2, Episcopal Day School
Ms. Garner, Teacher

And When the Sun Comes Up

When I was outside
it was early in the morning.
It was dark outside and stormy.
I was walking around the house
when there was a noise.
Whoosh!
It might have been the wind
or a ghost!
I was terrified!
Then, I heard another noise.
Thump!
It sounded like feet stomping.
I jumped up in terror.
Then, the Sun came up.
My mom said it's ok,
the sounds you heard were the wind
and the neighbor's dog.

GRADES 1 – 2
DIRECTORS SELECTION

Elle Palmer
Grade 2, Episcopal Day School
Ms. Caldwell, Teacher

Hiking Up the Valley

We went to a valley late at night
Hiking up the valley
It's a wonderful thing to see
The valley is as tan as the sand
Rocky as Old Smokey
I hear the rattle of the snake
I see the dust weeds tumble in the wind
I smell the dry clay of the valley
I taste the dust when I run in the valley
I feel the dust as hard as a rock
It is getting early
The sun was coming up like it was
coming up from bed
Carrying my bag and slumping down oh so sad
Suddenly I saw bright light
Roaring colors – pink, orange and more
It was the sun rising up from above

GRADES 1 – 2
DIRECTORS SELECTION

Wilmer Mitchell
Grade 2, Episcopal Day School
Ms. Caldwell, Teacher

Camping

Camping with my family
Hudson, Marian, Mom and Dad
We go on a hike
I see different birds
I see a lot of plants and animals
We hike up a mountain
I see flowers and insects
My legs hurt
I take a rest
I am very tired
I eat a snack
Then, I clean up after myself and go higher
At last, I am at the top.
I look down
I see homes, I see big, I see small
I see people
Then we go back down
We set up the tent
I go to sleep
I wake up early
It is still dark outside
I get out of my tent
I feel the bitter cold
I get dressed and walk up the mountain
Up, up to the top

When I get to the peak, the sun rises
I feel happy in my heart
I hear the birds chirping loud
I spot large mountains
I see rivers and lakes
It is warming up
I'm happier than before.
The sun is up – there is no more to see.

GRADES 1 – 2
DIRECTORS SELECTION

Kendall Skitt
Grade 2, Episcopal Day School
Ms. Garner, Teacher

The Rough Gulf

I was on my boat
with passengers who like to float.
The Gulf was very rough.
I was very tough.
Bump, Bump, Bump, Bump, Bump, Bump!
Maybe the Gulf was rougher than I was tough!
Then, I started to puke!
My passengers started screaming,
"Suck it up, buttercup!"
One of my passengers started crying.
So, I yelled, "Stop crying', dandelion!"
I said, "Let's go back."
Two of my passengers yelled, "No way, Jose!"
I still went back because I was ill.
I was ill so I took a pill.
I woke up, it was just a dream,
so I started to scream!
My mom came and said, "Take a chill pill."
So, I took one.
When I went to brush my teeth,
my Mom said, "Rinse, prince."
And then, the Sun came up.

GRADES 1 – 2
DIRECTORS SELECTION

Harper O'Hanlon
Grade 2, Episcopal Day School
Ms. Caldwell, Teacher

When the Sun Rises

When the sun rises,
it is peaceful.
It is very colorful
I walk outside
to see the sun come up.
I run up the hill.
The sun is bright like a lightbulb.
The sun rises too slowly.
I sit there very patiently
and watch the sun come up.
It peeked over the world.
It was so pretty.
It almost made me cry.
The sky's faint almost died.
The light shone on my face.
The sun peeks up over the valley.

GRADES 1 – 2
DIRECTORS SELECTION

Makaila Thomas
Grade 2, Episcopal Day School
Ms. Caldwell, Teacher

Ocean

An afternoon breeze blew calmly
Close to an ocean
It has sand as soft as a silk blanket
Meanwhile I watched the sun sleepily go down
Waves were calm
The wind gently blew
I felt relaxed as I sat under a palm tree
The next day I watched the sun happily rise
Above the deep blue sea
The sun looked at the world around it
The waves sadly waved goodbye to me
As I walked away from the magnificent ocean

3rd ~ 4th Grade Division

GRADES 3 – 4
1st PLACE

Katie Overholtz
Grade 3, Episcopal Day School
Ms. Taylor, Teacher

On a Sunny Day

On a sunny day

The Sun is out
Smell the flowers blooming,
Feel the breeze blowing
And hear the leaves moving.

Oooh, it feels hot
I need a cool drink
Pour some ice
Bang bang clink

Let's have some fun
It's a beautiful day
Grab a ball,
Let's go out and play!

Do you hear the ice cream truck?
I could taste vanilla topped with cherry
Maybe rocky road
Or even strawberry

It's getting dark
The stars shine bright

Let's go back inside
My teddy says "night night"

Now it's time
to close my eyes
I will see you sun,
when you rise.

GRADES 3 – 4
2nd PLACE

Kyrie King
Grade 4, N.B. Cook
Ms. Jackson, Teacher

Angel of the Night

Swoosh! Faster than a lightning bolt,
as beautiful as a young colt,
the owl swoops, catches its prey
and eats it in one gulp.

Snowy owls are the most beautiful I've seen
they fly and resemble Angel's wings.
I can't believe my eyes, like an Angel in disguise,
they are the guardians of the sky and my dreams.

When life is like the woods at night,
you're lonely, scared and full of fright,
and you may hear one call, "Hoo! Hoo!"
Fear not, behold the owl, he's a beautiful light.

Above the mountains the owl can see
my spirits sour high above the trees.
When the sun rises, the owl will rest his eyes
but his journey will always be with me.

GRADES 3 – 4
3rd PLACE

Alastair Casler
Grade 4, N.B. Cook
Ms. Ferrara, Teacher

Mysteries of the Deep

Swishing and swashing,
roaring and pouring.
Churning and turning
rising and diving up and down.
Stealing sand and land,
splashing and crashing on ships.
Deepening and darkening depths
hold many mysteries,
and then the sun rises,
revealing the sea.

GRADES 3 – 4
HONORABLE MENTION

Spencer Clark
Grade 4, N.B. Cook
Ms. Jackson, Teacher

Am I A Poet?

My mom says I can be a poet
and I don't even know it.
She says it's a little about rhyming,
but mostly about trying.
I don't know if that is true,
but for extra credit,
I must attempt to do.
So tonight I will try,
and when the sun rises,
I might not be able to deny,
I am a poet and didn't even know it.

GRADES 3 – 4
DIRECTORS SELECTION

Grace Timmons
Grade 4, N.B. Cook
Ms. Ferrara, Teacher

What It's Like

Living the life of a refugee
is not the way I want to be.
I'll lose my friends,
my home, my school and my hens.

With bombs exploding in the sky
and bullets zipping by,
I guess it's time
to say goodbye.

Too dangerous to stay.
I always pray
I will survive another day.

All will be different.
Everything – I'll miss.
Nothing will be the same
from glimmering stars to a
new friend's name.

War is chaotic,
even for animals that are aquatic.
I can never sleep
for I hear way more
than a peep.

Living the life of a refugee
is not the way I want to be.
Until the sun rises.

GRADES 3 – 4
DIRECTORS SELECTION

Camden Mandel
Grade 4, N.B. Cook
Ms. Jackson, Teacher

Sunrise

See all those thousands of smiles?
Under those smiles were bits of the sun.
No one can go close, only watch.
Rising, an experience inside of me.
I feel happy, peaceful and amazing.
Smells like the shiny beast is enjoying a feast.
Eating the darkness away.

GRADES 3 – 4
DIRECTORS SELECTION

Aubree Lowery
Grade 4, N.B. Cook
Ms. Ferrara, Teacher

The Sun Dances into the Sky

The sun dances into the sky,
turning on the light switch for the world.
Opening my eyes to say hello.
Slowly, the world is painted bright yellow.

The sun walks me through the day,
with a smile on her face.
Sadly when so tall in the sky,
she must start to say goodbye.

As she settles down,
the moon calls her name.
Even though she may slowly go away,
she never really says goodbye.

And I see her once again...
when the sun rises.

GRADES 3 – 4
DIRECTORS SELECTION

Arrianna Young
Grade 4, N.B. Cook
Ms. Jackson, Teacher

And When the Sun Rises

As flowers bloom
and the breeze gently flows;
morning is on its way.
The sweet smell of roses
tickles my nose
and the wind takes my worries away.
The morning brings a new beginning.
As I listen to the crickets sing
I stop and I think
about all that I'm thankful for
and all that I have
when the morning comes;
and the sun rises.

GRADES 3 – 4
DIRECTORS SELECTION

Mia Angeles
Grade 4, N.B. Cook
Ms. Jackson, Teacher

Sunshine

It's where the night
Turns into the day
Where the city comes awake
It's where the children start complaining
The adults start working
The teens start texting
The birds start chirping
The owls start sleeping
The fish start swimming
The cats start purring
The dogs start barking
The dolphins start flipping
The lions start roaring
The elephants start calling
The bears start fishing
Just thing
This all happens
Just when the sun rises

5th~6th Grade Division

GRADES 5 – 6
1st PLACE

Mason Juliusson
Grade 6, Ferry Pass Middle
Mr. Bridges, Teacher

The Shift from Darkness

Smashed window sound like a screeching cat,
murmurs of masked shadowy men
lie in the background,
tall building lights turn off one by one
as if they were being shot down,
the street lights falling shortly behind.

The silver projectile rises to the center
of the navy blue sky,
dents in it as if it were in a car crash,
a scream of high pitched voices
echoes through the skyscrapers,
but the color of a seashell
rises over the horizon like how
the light to heaven is in pictures.

The flare of luminous light
bursts from the center of
the solar system,
the darkness becoming less,
less,
less,
until shadows of emptiness is
all left behind.

What was depression and evil
is now sugar plums fairies dancing,
the navy blue now to a bright cyan,
what an awful place with the sunlight,
the thing that makes night good
is the fright.

GRADES 5 – 6
2nd PLACE

Tori Vinson
Grade 6, PATS Center
Ms. Haddocks, Teacher

And When the Sun Rises...

The moon cautiously gazes down on me,
its gentle beams daring to light up
my hair and hands.
It looks tired and worn,
puzzled by the events of the day before.
I wonder what tragedies it has witnessed,
what miracles it has observed.

The stars gravitate towards me excitedly,
twinkling, flashing and blinking.
Their beautiful patterns amaze me,
and remind me of the quilt on the bed
I should be on.
I contemplate the fact that as I write this sentence,
1800 of those wondrous stars are exploding.

Leaves rustle above me,
as a sturdy, wooden branch supports the swing
which I sit upon.
I hear buzzes around the pristine flow of the lantern,
promising insect life.
The moon kisses the tree,
leaving a speck of light for each leaf
to call its own.

I remember the day before.
The loneliness,
the shameful, melancholy memories.
Will the sun comfort me warmly,
or will the days before
only repeat?

In my books,
the sunrise is symbolic
for redemption,
for happiness,
for joy,
for rebirth.

But reality is not a book.
Will the sun light the way,
or hurt my eyes,
and expose the bruises
from the day before
that dominate my thoughts?

Reality is not a book.
And when the sun rises,
I will fade into the crowd once more.
But until the sun rises,
I shall be content,
and enjoy the night.

GRADES 5 – 6
3rd PLACE

Samantha Parris
Grade 5, N.B. Cook
Ms. King, Teacher

The Sun Rises

The sun rises like dust rising from the ground,
like flares of happiness it shoots up,
like an eagle soaring through the sky,
luminating the world it rises,
shining from east to west,
north to south,
warming your soul it rises,
the animals of the world bow down to it,
chasing darkness away for you it rises,
the sun is the king of earth,
it shines the way,
it brightens your day,
it warms like a summer week,
it will keep shining for you,
every day,
every week,
every month,
every year,
for as long as it takes,
it will not stop,
not for a second
it will rise
rise,
rise,
and rise.

GRADES 5 – 6
HONORABLE MENTION

Christian Huynh
Grade 6, Ferry Pass Middle
Mr. Bridges, Teacher

Elemental

Everything starts
dark as nothing itself.
A globe of light rises
and shimmers.
A big blob of
liquid fire
blazed in glory.
Shielded by layers of rock
and steel quarry.
A force field of air
and wind
surround
the rocky sphere.

Pools and pools
of water rain down
from a mere droplet
while the marshmallow
sky turns grey and roars.
Humongous islands form
and green life's
growth soars
and finishes the hard
work.

Mighty protectors
flesh and blood.
To grow and harvest
are home
time
by
time.

GRADES 5 – 6
DIRECTORS SELECTION

Gemma O'Day
Grade 5, EDS
Ms. Boyles, Teacher

Outer space

Sunrise
Sunset
Day
Night

Sun
Moon
Black
Pink

Sun dawning
Moon rising
Moon dawning
Sun rising

Sky
Full of
Colors
Newness
Hope
Love

Glimmering
Shining

Sparkling
Glistening

Stars shooting
Hesitating to move
Scared to be seen
Disappearing
Into Dust
Stardust

Galaxies above
Stare down
Watch

GRADES 5 – 6
DIRECTORS SELECTION

Kieyla Jones
Grade 5, Hellen Caro
Ms. Hahn, Teacher

What Happens When the Sun Rises?

What happens when the sun rises?
This always fills me with a sense of wonder.
When the gigantic burning ball of gas
rises over the horizon,
it wakes the world up from a long night of slumber.
An illusion created by earth to make it seem
like the sun is rising near,
a ray of white sunlight traveling
through the atmosphere.
Some colors scattered out by a beam
of air molecules, and tiny photons.
The light shines in the windows and
through the curtains.
But unfortunately the sun is not all day,
it is time for a new celestial being to come to play.
The moon comes out creating night,
yet we still have light.
The night is here, with balls of gas, out so far,
the moon and its sparkling, shiny stars.

GRADES 5 – 6
DIRECTORS SELECTION

Joone Kim
Grade 6, Ferry Pass Middle
Mr. Bridges, Teacher

Pitch Black

Break of dawn
darkness devours the auroral lights.
The only illumination are the twinkling stars
shadows roam freely,
when it's darker than a thief's pocket
people fear this opaque light
but I know I'm not afraid
because I will be rescued
by the break of day.

GRADES 5 – 6
DIRECTORS SELECTION

Victor Ceniceros
Grade 6, Ferry Pass Middle
Mr. Bridges, Teacher

When it Fades Away

In the horizon
A big ball of fire rises from the sky
It is known as the sun
It comes out and then it fades away
Every now and then

The creatures awake at the light of the sun
Knowing that day has finally come
But day doesn't always last
As always it soon fades away

The creatures scatter
They all hide away
As the white sun comes out to play
The white sun brings complete darkness and silence
As if the earth itself were a ghost town

But soon the sun will rise once again
And when the sun rises...
They will all come out.

GRADES 5 – 6
DIRECTORS SELECTION

Amelia Vines
Grade 6, Myrtle Grove Elem.
Ms. Brummet, Teacher

When the Sun Drops Gold

When the sun comes out it drops gold.
Through windows and curtains gold drops.
No matter what season it's still a golden sun.
For the sun is a flower and drops light from above.
It sparkles and gleams and gives a golden glow.
It gives light to children down below
to show the way.
The sun is a flower gleaming and
glistening and shining.
For the world down below to shine like beauty.
Even at night the sun still shining
when we cannot see it.
Bright as all the beauty in the world and more.
It is truly golden and beautiful and it
will always be bright.
Even though it's dark the sun is still there
when you need it the most.
We will never know truly why the sun is a
flower that glows from the sky.
All we know is gold is what drops for those below
in cities and towns.
The sun will always be there even at night
like a flower blossoming gold.

7th ~ 8th Grade Division

GRADES 7 – 8
1st PLACE

Trent Lowe
Grade 8, Little Flower School
Ms. Hughes, Teacher

All Lives Matter

Black lives and Blue lives,
Tall lives and Small lives
Sinners' lives and Saved lives,
Gay lives and Straight lives,
Old lives and Young lives,
Born lives and Unborn lives,
Law abiding lives and Criminal lives,
Students' lives and Teachers' lives,
Disabled lives and Able-bodied lives,
Genius lives and Learning impaired lives,
Humble lives and Boastful lives,
First World lives and Third World lives,
Believers' lives and Non-believers' lives,
Wealthy lives and Poor lives...

...All Lives Matter.

And when the sun rises,
I won't have to wear a t-shirt to remind you.

GRADES 7 – 8
2nd PLACE

Graybill Partington
Grade 8, EDS
Ms. Majors, Teacher

Sunny, My Days Are Now Darker

I still remember you clearly now,
your soft orange fur and your sweet "meow."
Every time I saw your dear fluffy face,
my loving heart began to quicken and race.

Then one day, our entire world fell,
what happened to you, we couldn't tell.
Your adorable smile began to fade,
your bright green eyes, no longer jade.

Two loose dogs attacked, they said,
you tried to run far far ahead
but they had the advantage
quickly causing great damage.

As the week crept on,
you fought to stay strong.
But sadly in the end,
we could no longer pretend.

Why did this happen?
We lost our dear friend,
why hurt our sweet pet?
Our family lost and upset.

Sometimes, I still see you,
when I am not trying to.
Around the corner and on the floor,
even peeking at the house door.

I am starting to see
that you will always be
there, when the sun rises,
and when there are blue skies.

You will be waiting there
with your soft orange hair.
Healed and happy too,
purring, "I love you."

GRADES 7 – 8
3rd PLACE

Gabrielle Vines
Grade 8, PATS Center
Ms. Haddocks, Teacher

A Sun Rises in War

It's a warm afternoon, with a blood soaked sky,
Colors of red, orange, pink and white,
Bombs drop and a dark haze surrounds
a dwindling sky,
Men lurk in the shadows armed with
guns and knives,
The children scream, but no one will look,
The city a warzone of pain and fear,
Homes going up in flames, consuming what's near,
Bodies piling up in sewers flooded by tears,
Humans fleeing, leaving a long flood trail behind,
Millions trapped, their lives on the line,
Escape is impossible without money and time,
Suspended in fear as they are stuck in the dust.

Night comes with more danger and death,
The grim reaper busy with the people that are left,
Hope demolished like the buildings
on every street,
Children knee deep in blood and war,
A city once beautiful, taken over by gore,
The night sky is filled by
explosions of light,
Screams and nightmares occupy the night,
The foundation crumbles and cracks,

Soon the city won't even have rats,
The wind whistles through abandoned streets,
Carrying poisonous gasses to all it meets.

And when the sun rises,
New bodies are found,
In smuggler vans, streets and other towns,
Children washed up on beaches and shores,
A generation lost to sorrow and decay,
Escape a horizon that will never be reached,
The people alive stranded in the sun,
Families weeping, the war isn't done,
Another day of death and loss will pass by,
People desperate, trying to make it out alive,
As the city of Aleppo,
Leaves a silence of the dead,
As the sounds of gunfire start up again.

GRADES 7 – 8
HONORABLE MENTION

Emily Doyle
Grade 7, EDS
Ms. Robinson, Teacher

Hurricane Katrina

I was too young to understand
These things don't happen everyday
They are not planned
The waves were rugged and fearless
The skies were unforgiving and dark
The first spark flew through the sky
I heard crashing and cries
I could see the fear in my family's eyes
I couldn't walk
I could barely talk
We were falling apart
So was the house
We packed our things
I turned around
I can imagine what happened
My home falling to the ground
I don't remember the rest of the story
Why would I?
A memory that dark and gory
This was long ago
Some houses are still ruined
That could've been mine
The thought of the feeling
Sent shivers down my spine

I want to get rid of the pictures in my brain
I hope this tragedy never happens again
This is what happens
When you get hit by a hurricane
The next day
Was a blue
We're back to where we began
A fresh start
When the sun rose that day
It filled the hole in my heart

GRADES 7 – 8
DIRECTORS SELECTION

James Young
Grade 7, EDS
Ms. Majors, Teacher

The Sun Rises

When night comes to an end the sun rises
I despise morning it means the darkness is ending

My soul feeds off the darkness at night
Pretending to let the light in breaks me
more and more

At school they ask how the day is you have to lie
and say it's good
It hurts to pretend that it's going well

It changes however when I see a person
that makes me happy
then I remember that I had hurt them before

I go home look at the sunset the highlight of my day
When the sun sets the moon comes out

I get to be my normal self no filters around
I let it all out and I get to feel better

I will myself to a sleep I thought I would hate
I dream good thoughts in my sleep,
first time in a while

When the sun rises in the morning I feel happier
I found that same person that made me happy

This time I care about them more than before
They had given me another chance

All of the stuff that happened in the darkness
There was no more

When the sun rises I am joyful and full with energy
And when the sun falls I still am

GRADES 7 – 8
DIRECTORS SELECTION

Ella Major
Grade 7, EDS
Ms. Robinson, Teacher

Untitled

At first people didn't know who you were
Know what you were
They studied you
They examined you
You felt lost
I could tell
I remember
I was there
They asked you questions
But you couldn't answer
You can't speak
You can't tell people what
your emotions are
And you can't speak your mind
You used your energy to explain
your feelings
Even if we don't know what
you're saying
If you're angry you flare up
It gets hot
If you're tired you hide
You go away
I wish you wouldn't do that
But you do
When you wake up you rise

You rise up and then wake me
I don't think I will ever understand
How you do it
Every day you get me through it
You are the reason I'm awake
Thank you

GRADES 7 – 8
DIRECTORS SELECTION

Allie Sinkovich
Grade 8, EDS
Ms. Majors, Teacher

You

As the sun rises, all I can think about is you
watching the flames crest the earth
I imagine reaching towards you.

Gazing at the crescent
of a brand new day
I wonder if I would see you.

Halfway above the earth
emitting streams of light
I know no matter how hard I try
I'll never be anything to you.

Emerging from the horizon
cascading the world
in colors of all kinds
I realize
the could never be as beautiful as you.

An angel ascending to heaven
the Sun rises
and in that moment I notice.
The similarities between it and you.

A blazing light
sucking all the attention to you
yet blowing life to everything near you
a color like no other
and you know there will never be a hue
quite like you.

And that's why
I could never have you.

GRADES 7 – 8
DIRECTORS SELECTION

Chris Moulton
Grade 7, EDS
Ms. Majors, Teacher

Morning at Belleau

The sun shone through and broke the
early morning fog.
The Devil Dogs were not quite done.
With a loud, "Ooh-Rah!" and fixed bayonets, they
charged towards the German machine gun nests.
The Germans looked up, "Teufelhunden!" they
cried, and all looked on with prying eyes.
They fumbled for their guns, but the Marines were
too quick, bodies were being stacked and the grass
was growing, the Marines were on a roll.
The Jerries used gas, the used artillery, but none of
these stopped the Marines.
Fritz was scared, he tried to surrender, little did he
know Devil Dogs take no prisoners.
They had the Germans on the run in the sun.
They abandoned their trenches, they dropped their
guns, they were all cowards.
The Marines charged the trenches and hurled
grenades, Fritz didn't stand a chance.
The Germans fled in every direction only to be cut
down by the Devil Dogs.
They underestimated the relentless hounds from
hell, and paid the price.

As Chesty Puller once said, "Hit hard, hit fast, hit often." Semper Fi they yelled, the day was won, and the sun shone on the victors.

GRADES 7 – 8
DIRECTORS SELECTION

Irelyn Thomson
Grade 7, EDS
Ms. Majors, Teacher

The Power of One

The Sun is one star
The Sun is one star out of 100 billion
stars in our galaxy
There are twenty-four times as many stars in the
universe than in our galaxy
The Sun is one star that is orbited
by nine planets
The planets are nine out of over 100 billion planets
in our galaxy
Earth is one planet in those nine
Earth has seven continents
Earth has 196 countries
Earth has 4,416 cities
Earth has seven billion people
living on it
There are twenty-three times as many planets in the
universe than in our galaxy
But when the sun rises on earth there are seven
billion people who matter
When the sun rises there are seven billion people
who need food
When the sun rises there are seven billion people
who need water
And when the sun rises there are seven billion
people who need love

You are one out of seven billion people
You are one person who needs food
You are one person who needs water
You are one person who needs love
You are one person who is loved

9th~10th Grade Division

GRADES 9 – 10
1st PLACE

Ari'abasi Jenkins
Grade 10, J.M. Tate High
Ms. Sarikaya, Teacher

The Sun Rises

It would have to shine. And burn. And be a sign of
something infinite and turn things and people
nearby into their wilder selves and be dangerous to
the ordinary nature of signs and glow like a tiny
hole in space

to which a god presses his eye and stares. Or her
eye. Some divine impossible stretch of the
imagination where *you* and I are one. It would have
to be something Marin Buber would say, seeing it,
point and rejoice.

It could be the mouth of a Coca-Cola bottle or two
snakes rolling down a mountain trail. It would have
to leap up out of the darkness of a theater and sing
the high silky operatic note of someone in love. And
run naked

slender fingers through the hair of a stranger, or
your mother or father, or grandfather, or a grassy
hill in West Virginia. It would live on berries and
moss like a deer and roam the woods at night like
the secret life of

the woods at night and when the sun rises you could
see it and think it is yours and that would be enough
and it would come to you

as these words have come to me—slowly,
tenderly, tangibly. Shy and meanderingly.

GRADES 9 – 10
2nd PLACE

Nashva Brouchton
Grade 9, J.M. Tate High
Ms. Sarikaya, Teacher

Traveling Bear

Grass blades push up between the cobblestones and
catch the sun on their flat sides shooting it back into
the eyes of passersby.
The legs of the bear shake and his back aches, and
the shining grass blades dazzle and confuse him.
But still he dances, because of
the little pointed stick.

GRADES 9 – 10
3rd PLACE

Gwendolyn Austin
Grade 10, J.M. Tate High
Ms. Moorehead, Teacher

As the Sun Rises

The world is woken with bittersweet
periwinkle skies,
as the moon and the stars whisper faintly
their last goodbyes.
The raindrops on our clumped eyelashes
romanticizes,
as the world soon stops for a moment
as the sun rises.

Only in that articulate instant of solitude,
in moments and seconds the world is
soon to be renewed.
Will we open our eyes too soon
when beauty capsizes?
As the world soon stops for a moment
as the sun rises.

The morning larks will shortly sing their
orchestrated songs,
and the dried up puddles will fill the void
of all our wrongs.
The clouds will go away and leave there our
compromises,
as the world soon stops for a moment
as the sun rises.

Before long moments and seconds will
turn into minutes,
and the hazy horizon will always test our limits.
We must learn to wake up and look past
the dark's disguises,
as the world soon stops for a moment
as the sun rises.

GRADES 9 – 10
HONORABLE MENTION

Michael Rogers III
Grade 9, J.M. Tate High
Ms. Pardue, Teacher

Cosmic Pantry

When the sun rises,
a billion explosions come into view,
as violent forces work in unison,
to keep the star there, in the sky.

Humanity,
the small creature that we are,
only wish to comprehend
this ball of fire in the sky.

But sadly,
this remains out of our grasp,
as though someone wants
its secrets to remain unknown.

But of course,
the sun is only one
star in the cosmic landscape,
surrounded by many different objects.

Stars,
however big they seem,
are only one of many
cosmological phenomenon's.

The cosmos,
a vast endless wasteland,
populated by many oddities,
many of which are yet to be discovered.

Hopefully,
when they are discovered,
maybe the sun will no longer be a mystery,
waiting to be solved.

The universe,
vast in size and scale,
larger than imagination itself,
contains our star.

Our universe,
one out of many possible,
but this one is ours,
and ours alone?

Dimensions,
they are large and mysterious,
unfathomable yet simple
yet understanding in unnecessary.

When will it happen,
when will we begin to understand,
our place amongst the stars,
let alone our own neighborhood.

The Pale Blue dot,
as Carl Sagan describes it,

is nothing but one chunk
of rock next to other rocks.

The Sun,
astronomers observe it,
physicists theorize about it,
and astrophysicists play with it.

It,
is still the unknown,
the final frontier,
the end goal for humanity.

Although,
as precious as it seems,
remember this,
it is still only one in trillions possible.

Formed,
billions of years ago,
in a cosmic mixing bowl,
the solar system was created, the sun its center.

The earth,
and its inhabitants,
are relatively new
in the place we call our home.

Are we alone?
Or are there others,
wanting to know more about their sun
waiting to be discovered

And until then,
the sun is still only a star
it is still only one of many,
beautiful structures in our dimension of reality.

GRADES 9 – 10
DIRECTORS SELECTION

Arianna Friedl
Grade 10, J.M. Tate High
Ms. MacDonald, Teacher

Everything Will Change

Night was the time when you complimented me.
Night was the time when you comforted me.
And when the sun rises, everything will change.
The moon rose as you held me in your arms.
The moon rose, and you told me I was beautiful.
And when the sun rises, you didn't talk to me.
The light in the sky fades, and you always
made sure that I'm okay.
The light in the sky fades, and you said
I was on your mind.
And when the sun rises, you claim
you didn't know me.
With the sun beneath the horizon, you said you
needed me in your life.
With the sun beneath the horizon, you held me close
as we danced the night away.
And when the sun rose, you took everything back.
Night is when you said nothing would change.
Night is when you said everything would be okay.
Night is when I kissed you.

Then night starts acting as if it were day.
Night turns into the time that we don't speak.
Night turns into the time that you ignore me.
And when the sun rises, everything is the same.

When the sun sets, you won't look me in the eyes.
When the sun sets, you act as if you hate me.
And when the sun rises, you turn your back on me.
The moon rose, and you ignore me
when I call to you.
The moon rose, and you aren't there to protect me
like you said you would be.
And when the sun rises, you ask about the scars, but
you don't realize you put them there.
The light is no longer in the sky, and
you push me away instead of hold me.
The light is no longer in the sky, and
you hurt me instead of comfort me.
And when the sun rises, will anything be
the way it was again?

GRADES 9 – 10
DIRECTORS SELECTION

Michelle Luther
Grade 10, J.M. Tate High
Ms. Young, Teacher

Last Goodbye

Sunlight is starting to reach the windows.
Lacing up worn shoes, dawn is telling me
I must leave.
The bag beside me brings tears to your eyes.
The reason behind my promise is
finally hitting you.
This is my last goodbye.
My time in this town has run out.
These restless bones aren't satisfied
pacing these streets anymore.
Dawn is reminding me of my way of life: a paper
bag flying away when the wind picks up.
Stubborn eyes, you're trying to follow me
through the deep snow.
I've stretched my time as long as
I could with you.
Soon I'll pass through the mountains, where you
won't be able to take another step with me.
My home is tied to the changing scenery while
yours is held together by these
structures and faces.
Your voice, wavering, is asking me
to turn around.
No matter how much you press on the paper, the
lines won't get any darker.

I'm wiping away the tears with chapped hands, your
wet sleeves making you shiver in the cold.
Leaving a shard of me in your pocket, I hope you
can remember the happiness you've made.
It's time to let me go.

GRADES 9 – 10
DIRECTORS SELECTION

Payton Conner
Grade 10, Pine Forest High
Mr. Copenhaver, Teacher

December 23rd

An arctic aesthetic masks the environment.
Shades of light blue, aqua and white
are visible from my window.
I walk out of my cabin home to
discover a diamond-like view.
The ground is layered with snow,
making it a blank canvas.
An overwhelming amount of ice is present.
The icicles in the doorway outside are
stalactites towering over me.
And when the sun rises…
The snow, the ice and the trees
become more breathtaking.
The smell of fresh pines add a relaxing aroma.
Today would be a pleasant day to go on a stroll.
However, I thought this should be a time to
script my thoughts.
As I hold a warm cup of tea, my mind is ready.
And the typewriter keys start clicking.

GRADES 9 – 10
DIRECTORS SELECTION

Tyteeyona Williams
Grade 9, J.M. Tate High
Ms. Sarikaya, Teacher

Messy Girls

Get up check your phone see what she posts on
social media screenshot send it to your friends tag
her in a post embarrass her on social media make
fun of her delete the comments walk in the kitchen
tell mom good morning get no reply get an apple go
to the bathroom stare at the self in the mirror look at
the girl picture look at her features and stare back at
yourself feeling ugly call friends talk about her go
comment nasty things under her picture ask her
questions antagonizing her tell her she's ugly make
her upset laugh with friends her dad a police officer
comes with all her friends and her you smirk
policeman ask you what happen you lie friends tell
on you lie and say they had no part in it you're
shocked your warned for cyberbullying she walks
off your friends laugh with her you look bad you
feel bad you call mom cry speak to mom get no
reply yell at her go to your room make a fake page
spill out all your friends secrets get blown up log off
page go to school.

11th ~ 12th Grade Division

GRADES 11 – 12
1st PLACE

Evelyn Odom
Grade 11, Pensacola High
Ms. Powers, Teacher

A View From the Heavens

A brush of Nyx's wings
and the lights go out. The children scream
but Morpheus comes and molds their dreams
and they sleep soundly.

Like souls in Asphodel,
on the alleys, those nameless, countless
wait for Thanatos in full darkness.
Completely silent.

Erebus covers them.
There's no sign, because they leave no trace,
except for Eos' tears the next day.
On the grass is dew.

Eos' tears are payment
for the righteous and the unrighteous.
Helios' rays fill worlds with brightness
the light shines for all.

Helios can cause pain
some crops grow, whereas others wither
unlike Dike, he deems no sinner
sun dries, not washes.

When Zeus releases rage,
sheltered ones don't see the blood wash away
because Iris, they think it's okay
it is a rainbow.

Mountains, Deucalion!
View this world like the deities do.

GRADES 11 – 12
2nd PLACE

Sal Caligiuri
Grade 11, J.M. Tate High
Ms. MacDonald, Teacher

And When the Sun Rises

The ones who come out at night are sometimes
the most amusing
The friends you make and the memories you try
to shake fall between the cracks
The city shines bright and the jazz blows
through the air
And when the sun rises the city dims.

GRADES 11 – 12
3rd PLACE

Lindsay Sharp
Grade 11, J.M. Tate High
Ms. MacDonald, Teacher

Love is the Thing with Daggers

Love is the thing with daggers
that resides in the heart,
and demonstrates the motions without divulging,
and never unremitting at all,

and trumpets in the mind is heard;
and thoughts must be the surge
that could execute the flaw
that stands inside us.

And when the sun rises
I've sensed it in the depths of my soul,
and uttered the words
yet, lust is demented with love,
it portrays its true self with time.

GRADES 11 – 12
HONORABLE MENTION

Leslee Scruggs
Grade 11, J.M. Tate High
Ms. MacDonald, Teacher

Night Game

As we step on to the field
we are judged by our performance.
Numbers on our back
and fear in our hearts.
As the sun goes down
and lights come on.
We dance in the night
with gloves in hand.
Catching flies with all the heat
hitting it hard to make it home.
Grass as green as the sky is blue
dirt as orange as the clouds are white.
Ball players come alive
when the sun goes down.
As the sun rises on another day
underneath the lights we want to play.

GRADES 11 – 12
DIRECTORS SELECTION

Hannah Lawerence
Grade 11, J.M. Tate High
Ms. Sarikaya, Teacher

My Sunrise

I used to look up to myself
I had a beautiful mind
But I'm losing that now
I'm losing what's mine

I don't know when it started
When I stopped being me
But all my broken pieces point
To my self-inflicted tragedy

I strangled my conscience
And tried to make it something new
But after all these years
She's finally broken through

Her voice is so loud
But I'm so far gone
My life is so dark
Because it's so close to its dawn

And today is the day
My hope ascends across the horizon
And I've thrown myself
Into the sun that is rising

I stand as it
Melts away the person I became
And I watch as it
Burns down the walls that I've made

And with nothing to hold me down
I will fly higher
I was made new
I was cleansed by fire

GRADES 11 – 12
DIRECTORS SELECTION

Kaylee Everett
Grade 11, J.M. Tate High
Ms. MacDonald, Teacher

Secrets

And when the sun rises
I know you'll no longer be mine
You'll leave my arms and go back
to your other life
You tell me you don't love her
And I'm the one for you
She has your days
I have your nights
She has your name and the ring
And I have your love
I know it's wrong but I can't help
but love you
I long for the day I can call you mine
For the days of
No secrets
No lies
No hurt
No pain
Just me and you
Our hearts as one
Til death does us apart
Until then our secret must remain
Between me and you just us two
I want that now but I know I must wait
So I'll wait for now

For the sun to set and for you to
find your way
Back to me
Holding me close and making me
fall more in love with you

GRADES 11 – 12
DIRECTORS SELECTION

Jennifer B. Repine
Grade 11, J.M. Tate High
Ms. MacDonald, Teacher

And When the Sun Rises

And when the sun rises
I think about my grandfather and his
battle with cancer
Limping like a homeless dog
Pain you cannot describe
Crawling for help
Do not know what to do
Collapsed to the ground
Leg snapped like a twig
Hoping to get better. He lay there still
Screeching ambulance sirens
Going into surgery thinking death
Replace a bone with cold metal
"Can I walk again?" soars through his mind
Learning to walk again is like
Teaching penguins to fly
Weak as a starving dog
Sitting in a wheelchair wishing he
Did not have cancer
Building his muscles day in and day out
Sore as a bone gnawed on for weeks
Leaving rehab as happy as can be
Being reunited with his family
He still thinks and wonders,
"will my life ever be normal again?"

Radiate his leg to kill cancer
Losing his hair like a shaved sheep
Going to be like this way for years
Hoping to get better
We wait and see
And when the sun rises
He is nowhere in sight

GRADES 11 – 12
DIRECTORS SELECTION

Samantha Harrell
Grade 11, J.M. Tate High
Ms. MacDonald, Teacher

Frenemies

Depression and anxiety have become
my new best friends
Both of them always bundled up in my tiny head
screaming at me
Me never knowing when I was going to have my
next break down
Slowly my body being changed from a beautiful,
olive, lively skin tone to a rough, pale,
lifeless skin tone
Never being able to get an hour or even a minute of
sleep or even an ounce of food
And when the sun rises and you are next to me
happiness and pure joy became my new best friend

GRADES 11 – 12
DIRECTORS SELECTION

James Jordan-Ward
Grade 11, J.M. Tate High
Ms. MacDonald, Teacher

And When the Sun Rises

And when the sun rises...
I'll be back home
all these bad memories will be long gone.
I'll wake up in the morning with a smile on my face
knowing that I'm loved, knowing that I'm safe.
I've waited for this all my life
To have a family, is a dream of mine.
All I've known is one house to another
But all I want is to be with my mother.
Many a time I've sat and cried
Pondered things and asked myself why...
Why does it have to be this way
They left me here with nothing to say.
I've made it through many sad tears
I can be strong for many more years.
I haven't been alone this whole time
I've had someone by my side.
He died for me, so I live for him
He loves me as much as my mama did.
And when the sun rises and my time ends
I'll be so glad to see my mama again

GRADES 11 – 12
DIRECTORS SELECTION

James Chism
Grade 11, J.M. Tate High
Ms. MacDonald, Teacher

Resurrection

And when the sun rises,
The knight shall rise
From his abysmal existence.
Broken and bloodied by pain,
He shall finally be released
By this newly rising sun.
He would be resurrected
From this sorry hollowed state.
In this land of hollows
He would vanquish the demons
And destroy machinations
Of fallen gods.
Destroyer or savior,
This was left in the eye of the beholder.
Let the sun shine upon this Lord of Cinder.

So you want to be a Writer

"if it doesn't come bursting out of you
in spite of everything,
don't do it…
don't be like so many writers,
don't be like so many thousands of
people who call themselves writers,
don't be dull and boring and
pretentious, don't be consumed with
self-love.
the libraries of the world have
yawned themselves to
sleep…
don't do it.
unless it comes out of
your soul like a rocket,
unless being still would
drive you to madness…
don't do it.
unless the sun inside you is
burning your gut,
don't do it.

when it is truly time,
and if you have been chosen,
it will do it by
itself and it will keep on doing it
until you die or it dies in you.

there is no other way.

and there never was."

-Charles Bukowski

And When the Sun Rises…

51745140R00062

Made in the USA
San Bernardino, CA
31 July 2017